SOULS ON FIRE

Inspired Writings
By
Sandra J Yearman

SERAPHIM PUBLISHING LLC

WE WILL BRING LIGHT TO ALL THE DARK PLACES

Registered trademark-
Sandra J Yearman
Seraphim Publishing
438 Water St. Cambridge, WI 53523

Library of Congress Control Number: 2009907414
ISBN: 978-0-9841506-0-1
First Edition

Let The Spirit Fill The Conscious
Let The Spirit Fill The Souls
Let The Holy Spirit Pour Forth
Through Eternity To Toll
Amen
Amen
Amen

CONTENTS

DEDICATION

SEEKING LIGHT IN THE DARKNESS

CONTENTS

COMING HOME

Dedication

Holy Spirit

In all the worlds that ever were
In all the worlds that ever will be
Let Your Name ring through eternity
Let praises be sung to Thee

Let the Spirit fill the conscious
Let the Spirit fill the souls
Let the Holy Song pour forth
Through eternity to toll

Consume us with Your Presence
Consume us with Your Peace
Consume us with Your Love
Your Holy Word to feast

Amen Amen Amen

The Sound Of Holiness

Would we recognize the sound of
Holiness
A sound we have heard before

God spoke to us in a whisper
And the whisper grew to a roar

The Word walked among us
And blessed us with His Grace

The Word stood before us
And our darkness He did face

The Word conquered the dark worlds
And sowed God's Heavenly seeds

He healed our human frailties
And surrendered on His knees

To God the Lord and Father
The Creator of us all

To God who sent Him
To tear down the demon walls

God the Holy Spirit
God the Three in One
God the Blessed Word
God the Holy Son

Amen Amen Amen

The Song Of The Ages

You must have an open heart
To hear the Song of God

The Song we had forgotten
The Song we can never forget
The Song of the ages

The Eternal Song
That is sung by all creation

The Song that fills both the hearts of
Angels and of men

The Song of Truth and Light
The Song of Love and Mercy

The Song that originates all

Lord most Holy God

Open our hearts
That we may hear Your Song

Bless our voices
That we may sing Your Song

Cleanse our beings
That we may be consumed with Your
Song

Lord forgive us
And Bless us with Your Song

Amen Amen Amen

God Will Carry Me

One candle will light the darkness
One voice will fill the void
One prayer will be answered
God will carry me

If only one voice has the faith of many
If only one soul surrenders all
The dark walls will tumble down
God will carry me

If only one voice stands up to darkness
If only one voice says 'it stops now'
The horror, the terror, the injustice
God will carry me

One candle will light the darkness
One voice will fill the void
One prayer will be answered
God will carry me

With Faith miracles can happen

With Faith the boundaries are
overcome

With Faith the illusions are no more

God will carry me

Amen Amen Amen

You Are The All

You are the All
You are the Everlasting
You are Life without end

I will kneel at Your feet
I will believe
I will have faith

You are the Answer
You are the Source
You are the Song

I will worship You my God
I will sing Your Song
My being will be filled with
Your Presence

You are the Heavenly Father
You are the Holy Son
You are the Holy Host

I will worship You my Lord
I will honor You with my devotion
I will love You always

Amen Amen Amen

Glory

To the Glory of the Father
To the Glory of the Son
To the Glory of the Holy Spirit
Three in One

To the majesty of Heaven
To the majesty of Love
To the majesty of Peace
Gifts sent from above

God Bless us with Salvation
Bless us Your Peace
Bless us with Redemption
Our Holiness increase

God Bless us with Forgiveness
Cleanse us with Your Light
Bless us with Healing
Save us with Your Might

Holy Holy Holy is Your Name

Amen Amen Amen

Seeking Light In The Darkness

Deliver Us Home

Heavenly Father

Deliver us from darkness
Deliver us from illusions
Deliver us from sin
And deliver us Home

Guide us through this life
Direct our thoughts and actions
Carry our souls
And deliver us Home

Ignite the Will of God within us
Teach us to pray
Bless us with Your Majesty
And deliver us Home

Amen Amen Amen

Her Ways

Her voice was weak from hunger
With love it grew strong
The beauty of this creation
Was sang in loving song

And God, He sends us Angels
To guide us on our way
To stay with us in darkness
To turn the night to day

Tiny was her body
Courageous was her soul
She walked among the lions
She paid every earthly toll

Loyalty was her namesake
Graceful were her ways
God, I will thank You always
Until the end of days

For the lights You send to this world
For the miracles that are friends
Who arrive with perfect timing
To save us from our ends

Lord thank You for Your timing
Lord thank You for Your Grace
Thank You for the Miracles
You send into this place

Amen Amen Amen

Holy Warrior Rides

God sent forth an army
This world has never seen
An army without rest
Led by a Holy King

The army marched to the Song of
Faith
The strongest power known
God carried them in battle
God carried them to their Heavenly
Home

God in all His Holiness
And Heaven with all its Might
Stood before a dying world
And darkness lost the fight

Great armies they defeated
The dark fortresses could not stand
Before the Spirit of the Lord
And the Holiest King in all the land

In His understanding
God blessed this holy man
Who fought with faith and courage
And love songs to God he sang

God in all His Holiness
And Heaven with all its Might
Stood before a dying world
And darkness lost the fight

The army rode for justice
The army took a stand
To save the world from darkness
Every woman, child and man

The banner they rode under
The shield that stood before
God blessed them and saved them
And His Holy army soared

God in all His Holiness
And Heaven with all its Might
Stood before a dying world
And darkness lost the fight

The child king defeated giants
Because he surrendered to his Lord
His body had no boundaries
His holy spirit soared

The Angels heralded the coming
The demons fought with all their
might
The Song of God poured forth
Bringing Heaven's Holy Light

God in all His Holiness
And Heaven with all its Might
Stood before a dying world
And darkness lost the fight

In these days of turmoil
In these days of strife
The strongest weapon we can have
Is God within our life

The Holiest of warriors
Prevails unto this day
The Holy Angels of the Lord
Will help make a better Way

Amen Amen Amen

Gun And Crossbow

They took his gun and crossbow
And tried to make a cross
To signify the dead
Another life was lost

And the wars go through the ages
So many lives are lost
As their comrades take their weapons
And try to make a cross

The wind blows sand forever
And covers bodies where
No one will ever find them
Or know that they were there

And the wars go through the ages
So many lives are lost
As their comrades take their weapons
And try to make a cross

Do we ever learn our lessons
Do we ever listen to the wind
And hear the Angels tell us
Let go of your fear and sin

And the wars go through the ages
So many lives are lost
As their comrades take their weapons
And try to make a cross

We kill to fight for freedom
We kill to acquire land
We kill because our darkness
Terrorizes man

And the wars go through the ages
So many lives are lost
As their comrades take their weapons
And try to make a cross

We kill to fight for people
In wars created by the insane
Because of hate and fear
To glorify their names

And the wars go through the ages
So many lives are lost
As their comrades take their weapons
And try to make a cross

God deliver us with Mercy
Save us from this hell
Bring sanity to the living
Cleanse the darkness from where we
dwell

Amen Amen Amen

God Give Me The Words

God give me the words to heal this
world
To bring relief to the suffering
To bring Hope to the forgotten
To bring Your Light to all the
dark places

God give me the words to stop the
wars
To save the starving
To feed the hungry
To bring Your Peace to all the
dark places

God give me the words to help man
understand
To help them overcome their fears and
hatred
To help them see the Holiness in all
Your creations
To bring Your Love to all the
dark places

God give me the words, that I may
teach the world
That I may help others find their way
to You
That I may help others to hold onto
their faith

That I may ...

Amen Amen Amen

Nameless Cries

The nameless cries
The tortured souls
The overwhelming pain

Screams in the darkness
Chaos
Fear

The fires of hell burn
Is there any place to flee
Is there any escape

Our Heavenly Father please deliver
Us from these hells we have created

Deliver us from the chaos and fear
Deliver us from the pain and torture
Deliver us from ourselves

Please Heavenly Father
Save us
Forgive us
And bring us Home

Amen Amen Amen

I Am Crippled By My Fears

God please forgive me for the sins I
have committed against You
Against others
Against myself

Lord I need Your help
I need Your Faith
I need Your guidance

I am crippled by my fears
I have allowed the darkness within me
to control and ruin my life
I have worshipped idols of this world, I
have been destroyed

Lord I am so afraid of the darkness
I am afraid of my life
I am afraid of myself

God please rescue me
God please heal me
God help me to conquer my fears
God help me to cleanse the darkness
from my soul

God please forgive me and bless me

Amen Amen Amen

What World

The Father sells the children
And sins and sins again
What horror do they perpetuate
What world do we live in

Expose the demons that surround us
Rein their power in
Bring Holiness back to this world
Cleanse us of our sin

Conquer the darkness within us
Save us from ourselves
Bring Your Spirit within us
Remind us of Your Love

Surround us with Your White Light
Protect us with Your Grace
Cleanse us with Your Spirit
Bring balance to this place

Forgive us for our horror
Forgive us for our greed
Forgive us for our murders
And our unholy deeds

Help us to overcome our fears
To stand without disgrace
To call upon Your Holiness
To bring Heaven to this place

Amen Amen Amen

A Light In Every Storm

Darkness may over take us
And blind us in the night
Tossed on seas of confusion
Terrorized with fright

Numb to all the chaos
Tossed among the seas
Strong holds that were loosened
Lost and utterly

Sinking in the murky darkness
Overwhelmed by the gale
Look up to the Heavens
Ask to walk God's trail

Ask Him to pull you from the murky
waters
Ask Him to calm the storm
Ask Him to send you a Light
Ask Him to bring you Home

Amen Amen Amen

Lord Please Rescue Me

Lord I am imprisoned by my own fears
The walls are insurmountable to me
I can not escape without Your help

Lord I am so weak
I am so broken
I am dying

Lord I do not want to die alone

Lord please free me from my prison
cell
I can not see the path to freedom
I can not see in this darkness

Lord please save me
Please forgive me
Please have Mercy upon me

Amen Amen Amen

His Life

They said that he was crazy
They said that he was fun
The friend that Heaven sent me
A gift from the Holy One

He walked to his own drummer
He sang to his own song
He forgave the world around him
For he had been greatly wronged

He filled this world with laughter
He filled this world with life
He brought me many blessings
That I needed in my life

And when his life was ended
So short and so fleet
He left here as a warrior
An honor I would meet

He overcame the boundaries
Of a body filled with pain
He walked away with Glory
His Holy Home to gain

Amen Amen Amen

Our Fears

God cleanse us and help us to
overcome our fears
As individuals
As a people
As a world

Our fears consume us
Our fears destroy us
Our fears betray us

Our fears distort our realities
Our fears immobilize us
Our fears prevent us from
experiencing true love

Our fears prevent us from surrendering to our God

God heal us and heal the worlds we live in

Amen Amen Amen

The One Who Sacrificed

The one who sacrificed herself
Which was the ultimate test
She soared above the darkness within
So she could soar above the rest

There is no life so darkened
With pain and insanity
That miracles can not happen
When a voice cries out to Thee

Filled with many demons
Gnarled by all the pain
A love she was in my life
A blessing I did gain

To see behind the death masks
The Holy Flame that barely exists
Is worth the time and trouble
To prevent it from being extinguished

Like fireworks in the night sky
She filled this world with light
The friend of mine, who sacrificed
herself
To conquer the demons of the night

Amen Amen Amen

God Sent Down Fire

God's Holy messengers called out
His Name
'Lord help Your children to be saved'
And with faith they were inspired
The day God sent down His Holy Fire

God sent His Holy messengers
To show us Heaven's Light
To teach us and to heal us
To bring us from the night

But in our ignorance
To darkness we do cling
We listen to the demons
Our destruction we do bring

God's Holy messengers called out
His Name
'Lord help Your children to be saved'
And with faith they were inspired
The day God sent down His Holy Fire

God's Holy messengers
Cried with shame
At a world that had forgotten
God's Holy Name

Even though His children turned Him
away
God said 'with you I will always stay'
And though His children chose to die
God sent His Holy Fire from the sky

God's Holy messengers called out
His Name
'Lord help your children to be saved'
And with faith they were inspired
The day God sent down His Holy Fire

God's Holy Fire turned night into day
God's Holy Fire filled us with His
Light
God's Holy Fire showed us Gods'
Way
God's Holy Fire cleansed us from our
plight

And His children were inspired
The day God sent down His Holy Fire

Amen Amen Amen

Lost

The Holy Spirit
Is the answer
To all the questions
To all the problems
To all...

The Holiest Host
Is the reason
Is the cause
Is the Glory
Is the All...

Holy One
Carry us
Anoint us
Bring us Home

Holy One
Ignite the passion
Ignite the faith
Ignite the love
Of Heaven within us

Holy One
Take our hands
Breathe life into us
And help us to sing
Your Love Song through eternity

Amen Amen Amen

Into Your Light

Holy One please dissolve the darkness
that separates us
Help me to tear down the walls I hide
behind
Help me to stop creating barriers
between us

Holy One please help me to overcome
the fears that keep me from
surrendering to You

Help me to walk into Your Light

Holy One
Teach me to pray
That I might live again

Amen Amen Amen

The Cord Of Faith

Lord I am drowning in this dark world
I need something Holy to cling to
I need something Holy to save me

Lord send me a golden cord from
Heaven
To cling to until I return Home

Lord send me a golden cord from
Heaven
To grasp onto, so that I do not drown
In this current of darkness

Lord send me a golden cord from
Heaven
To clutch onto during this difficult
journey

Lord when the way is dark, I will cling
to my cord

Lord when I am frail, the cord will
sustain me

Lord when I have lost my way the cord
will show me the path to Heaven

Lord I will follow this cord Home

Amen Amen Amen

Through The Madness

The rescuers ran into horror
To save the victims there
But they can not escape the darkness
The terror that they share

Horrified by the carnage
That the demons leave in their wake
They strive to control the darkness
For all creations sake

God carry us from this madness
Calm the stormy seas
Save us from the demons
We pray upon our knees

That You will protect us in these dark times
No matter where we hide
Save the world You created
Change this deadly tide

Amen Amen Amen

Those Who Turn To Darkness

Why do people turn to demons
To give them power and might
Do they not understand
There is no power in the night

Light dissolves the darkness
Healing conquers pain
Faith overcomes the fears
From darkness there is nothing to gain

False light is no substitute
For the brilliance of the Son
In a war that has been fought
In a battle that has been won

God is the Power
Glory and the Grace
Darkness has no hold
If you ask to seek God's Face

Amen Amen Amen

Help Me To Conquer

Holy One
Help me to conquer
The fears that torture me
The darkness that controls my life
The pain and the agony

Holy One
I am so filled with anger and fear
With hatred and jealousy
With demons

Holy One
Help me to conquer
What I have created
What I have made as my own death
sentence
What I have chosen as my own prison

Holy One
Help me to conquer
I am so broken
So shattered
So weak

Holy One
I choose life
I choose light
I choose You

Amen Amen Amen

A World Gone Mad

People calling to darkness
And allowing it to take control

People calling to darkness
And allowing it to consume them

People calling to darkness
And losing their souls

What horror do we bring upon
ourselves
What death, what sins

The darkness is out of control
And our fears empower it

The darkness is out of control
And those who thought they could
control it are dead

The darkness is out of control
Please Lord save us all

Amen Amen Amen

Coming Home

A Ransom Paid

The bowels of the earth shook from
the thunder
As the miracles occurred
The voices of the Angels
In all the worlds were heard

As the Son of God defeated
The darkest demons known
And showered all creation
With forgiveness, with a Home

Darkness grew in the world
As the Spirit left the man
Allowing the prophesies to be fulfilled
By the Heavenly Father's Holy Hand

The armies of the demons
Thought they had won
Little did they realize
In that human vessel was God's
Holy Son

Light dissolves the darkness
As is the Holy test
The Father saved His children
The righteous and the blessed

For who so ever believeth
In the Father and in the Son
Is saved and Blessed by Heaven
A ransom paid by the Holy One

Amen Amen Amen

Let Us Celebrate With Joy

God is love
Let us sing and dance
Let the Holy Spirit move us

God is all
We are filled with life
We are filled with love
Let the Holy Spirit move us

Our voices are filled with song
We are singing praises to our God
Our tears flow
Let the Holy Spirit move us

God fill us with Your Presence
That every moment may be a
celebration
Of joy
Of love
Of life

God fill us with Your Presence
And let the Holy Spirit move us

Amen Amen Amen

His Holiness

Through eternity let Your Name be
praised
For You are the Salvation
For You are the Glory
For You are the All

Through eternity let us be filled with
Your Holiness
For You are our Peace
For You are our Redemption
For You are our Lord

Through eternity let us remember
Your promises and Your gifts
For You are the Holy Sacrificial Lamb
For You are the conqueror of
Darkness
For You are the Holy Son

Amen Amen Amen

Beyond Infinity

The Great I AM
All
Eternal
Without boundaries

The Word
The Source
The Song
Without definition

Love
Grace
Forgiveness

Man tries to contain that which is
beyond understanding
Man tries to explain the Divine
Man seeks what is with him always

Faith is the answer to the mysteries
Forgiveness a key
Forever is God

Amen Amen Amen

Chalice Of Fire

Chalice of Fire
Holy desire

Communion with Thee
Redemption for me

This is the hour
To touch Divine power

The Shepherd and sheep
His promises to keep

Shepherd and Lamb
The Great I AM

Staff and Crown
Holiness abound

Chalice of Fire
Holy desire

Amen Amen Amen

The Gift Of The King

The Gift of the King
To a world without reason

A Promise made flesh
To the un-accepting masses

The Word of the Divine
The Light of the ages
The Lamb of the Shepherd
The Warrior of the ancients

The Son of God
Timeless
Eternal
With us always

Amen Amen Amen

His Presence

I have witnessed miracles
Though they go untold
For those who do not seek
The mysteries do not unfold

I have asked that my sight not be
clouded
That I can see more than what is
before my eyes
I have been blessed by Mercy and
Grace
As God pierces the darkness and lies

Answers are for the asking
Kneel with Holy prayer
Talk to God
His Presence will be there

Amen Amen Amen

They Were Inspired
The Day God Sent Down
His Holy Fire
Amen
Amen
Amen